FLOWERS

Anna Pomaska

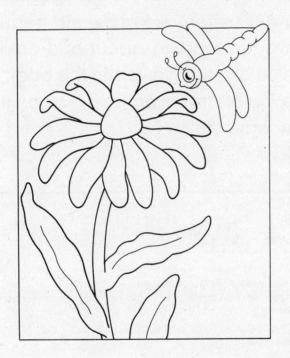

DOVER PUBLICATIONS, INC.
Mineola, New York

Note

You can find flowers just about everywhere—in parks, fields, your own garden or yard, even in flowerpots on windowsills. Flowers come in many sizes, shapes, and colors. They're fun to look at and many smell good, too. Flowers help make our world beautiful. Have fun reading about and coloring the 30 different flowers in this book. Use the colors mentioned or color them any way you like!

Bibliographical Note

Flowers is a new work, first published by Dover Publications, Inc., in 2000.

DOVER *Pictorial Archive* SERIES

International Standard Book Number: 0-486-41028-5

Manufactured in the United States of America
Dover Publications, Inc., 31 East 2nd Street, Mineola, N.Y. 11501

Rose

The ROSE is one of the most popular flowers. Red is the favorite color for roses, but they can be yellow, white, pink, orange, and other colors, too.

Crocus

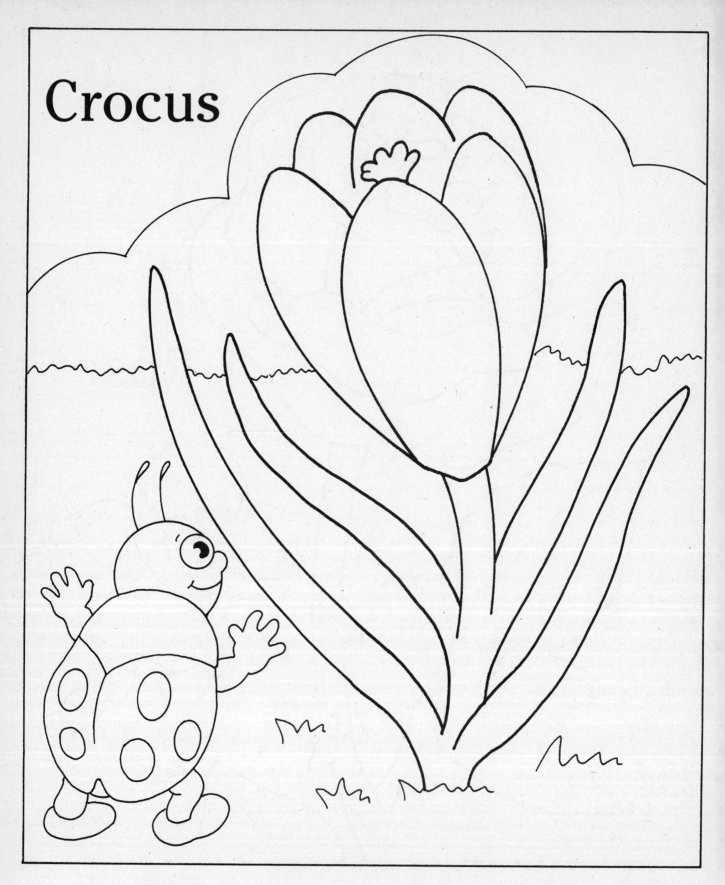

The CROCUS is one of the first flowers you see
in the spring. It can be purple, yellow,
pink, and other colors.

Bluebell

This small flower is shaped like a bell and is usually blue. That's why it's called the BLUEBELL.

Tulip

The TULIP comes in many colors. Sometimes the petals are several different colors at once. Many tulips are grown in Holland.

Daisy

You've probably seen this white and yellow flower.
It is the DAISY. It grows in fields and meadows.

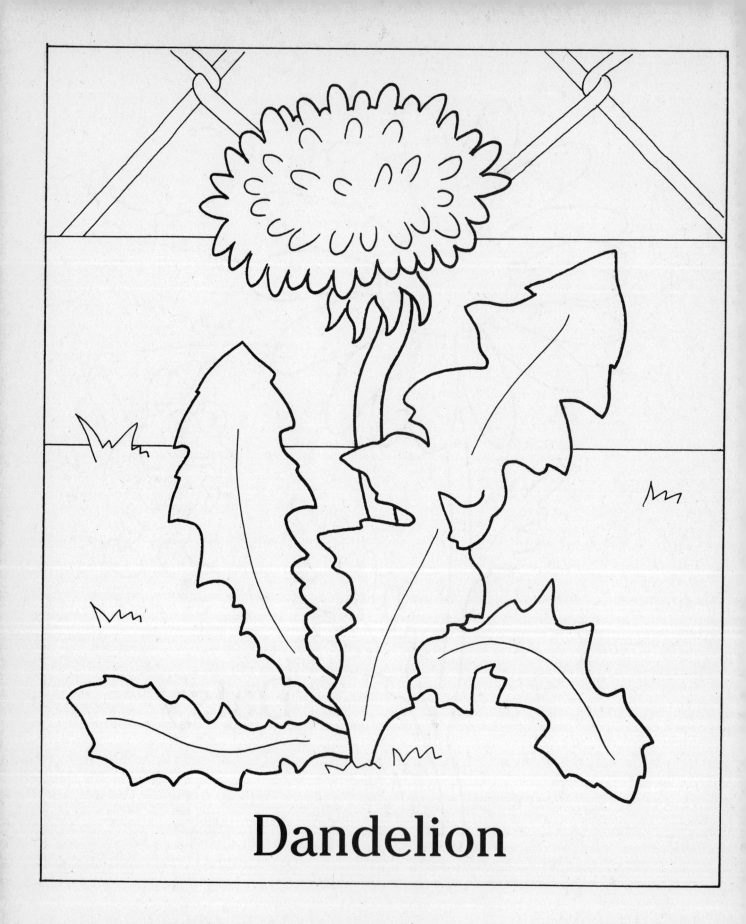

Dandelion

The DANDELION is bright yellow with broad green
leaves. It is really a weed, not a flower.

Morning Glory

Purple, pink, white, or a combination of colors, the
MORNING GLORY opens up in the morning
sun and closes by late afternoon.

Daffodil

This springtime flower is the DAFFODIL.
It can be orange, yellow, or white.

Iris

The IRIS is named for the Greek goddess of the
rainbow, and it can be just as many colors.

Cactus
Flower

The CACTUS FLOWER grows on cactus plants in hot, dry deserts. Many are pink, red, white, or yellow.

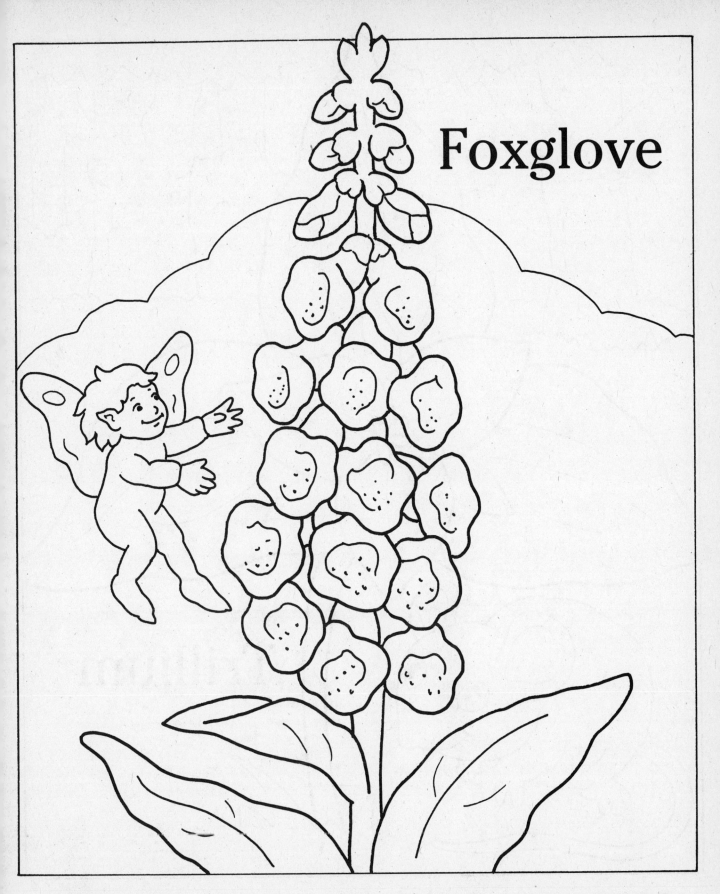

Foxglove

White, pink, red, or purple, this flower was named
FOXGLOVE because people once thought that fairies
gave them to foxes to wear as gloves.

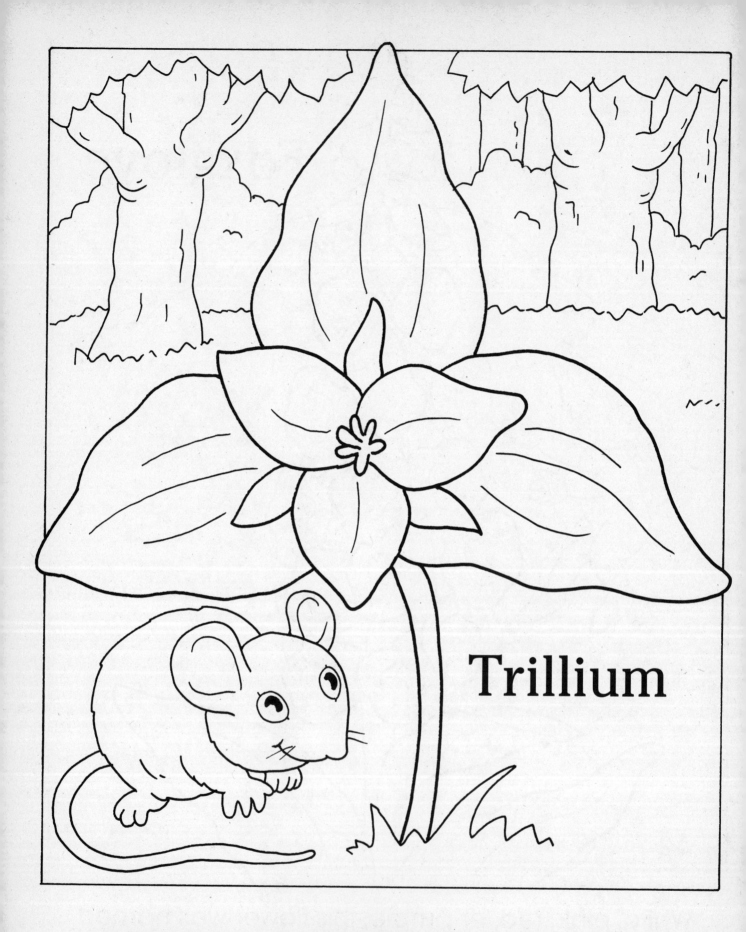

Trillium

The white or pink TRILLIUM grows in the woods.
It always has three leaves and three petals.

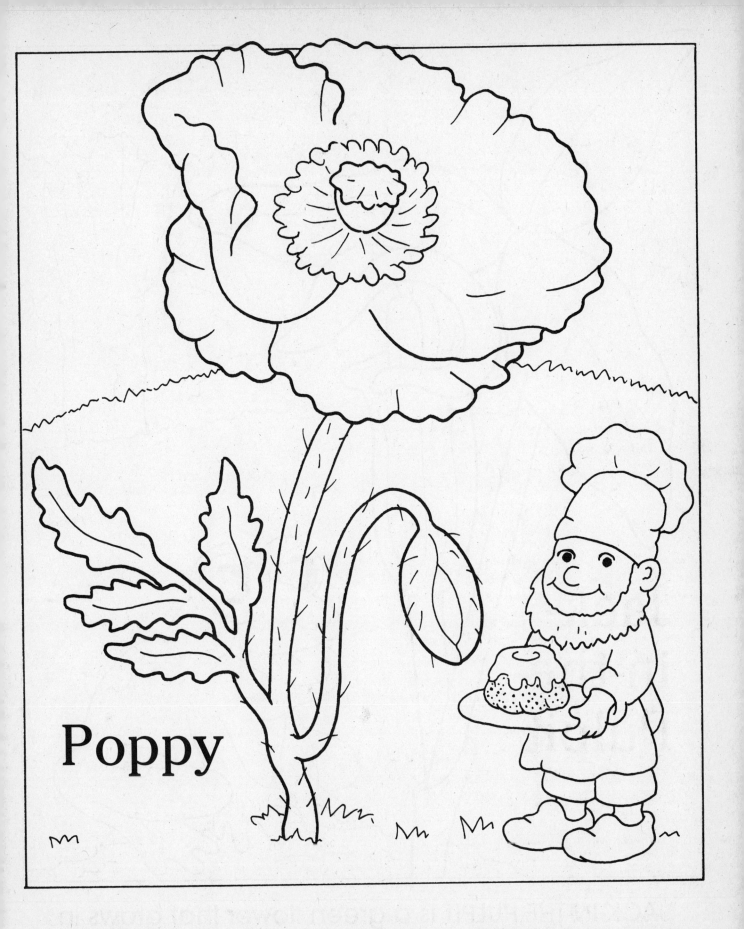

Poppy

The POPPY has bright red flowers and grows in fields.
The seeds can be baked in muffins and breads.

Jack-in-the-Pulpit

JACK-IN-THE-PULPIT is a green flower that grows in damp woods. It reminds some people of a minister standing in a church pulpit.

Columbine

The COLUMBINE has red and yellow drooping flowers. It grows in rocky and wooded places.

Hibiscus

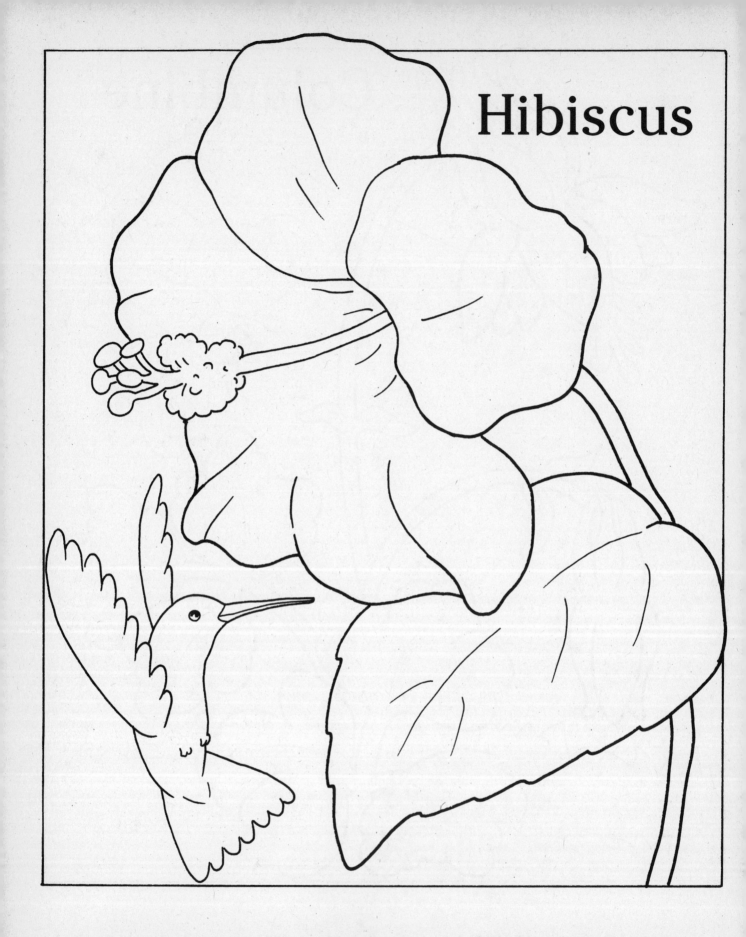

Growing in marshes and swamp areas, the lovely
HIBISCUS has large red petals.

Marigold

The MARIGOLD can be golden yellow, orange, or red. It grows well in the garden and in flowerpots, too.

Periwinkle

The PERIWINKLE is usually blue and grows best in shady places.

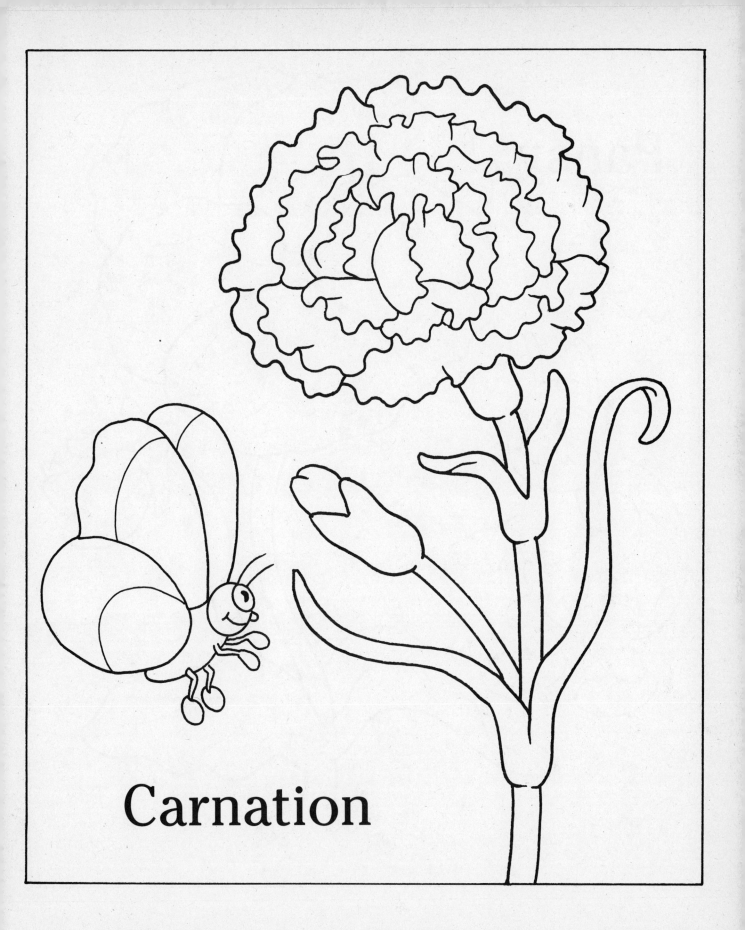

Carnation

The CARNATION can be red, pink, white, or a mix of colors. It is a favorite flower to use in bouquets.

Pansy

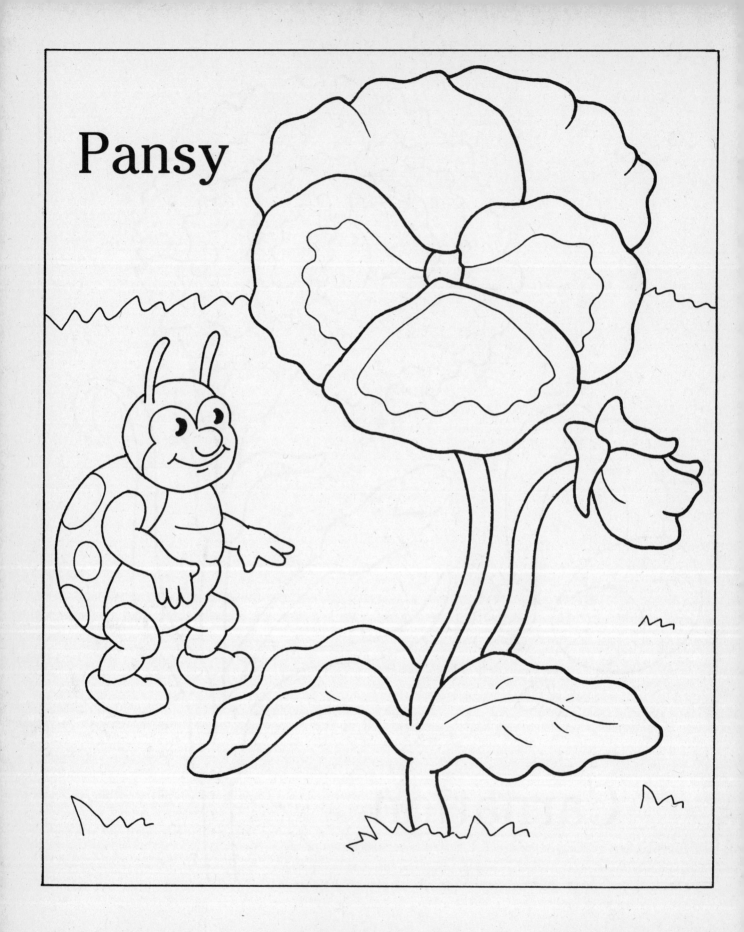

The PANSY is a colorful spring flower. It can be red, purple, yellow, or blue with dark markings.

Snowdrop

The white SNOWDROP grows in damp wooded areas. It can even grow in the snow!

Black-Eyed Susan

The BLACK-EYED SUSAN has yellow petals and a black or dark-brown center. It grows in fields and meadows.

Orchid

The ORCHID comes in many colors and grows in tropical jungles. It is often used in bouquets and corsages.

Evening Primrose

The EVENING PRIMROSE is a yellow flower that opens its petals at night. Its sweet fragrance attracts moths.

Violet

The lovely VIOLET can be reddish blue or other colors. Some states have made it their state flower.

Bird-of-Paradise

A tropical flower, the beautiful BIRD-OF-PARADISE
looks like a bird with bright orange and
blue head feathers.

Cyclamen

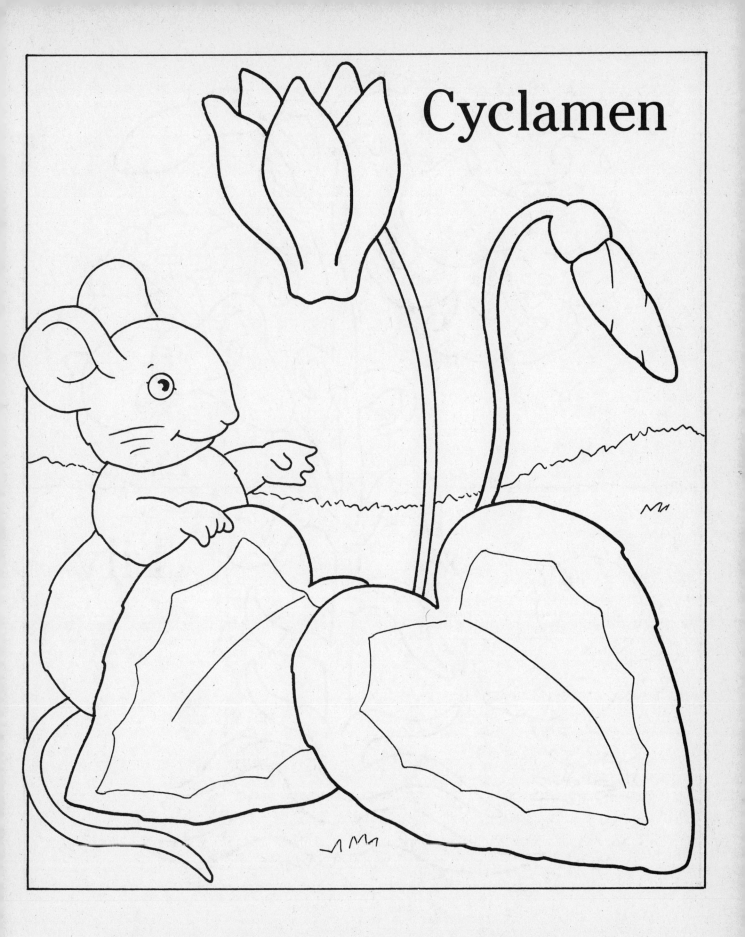

A pretty pink flower that grows well in the shade,
the CYCLAMEN has broad green leaves.

Lily

The LILY is a large flower that comes in many colors.
The white one is especially popular at Easter time.

Water Lily

Floating in a quiet pond, the WATER LILY can be
white, pink, yellow, or other colors.

Sunflower

The large, bright yellow SUNFLOWER can grow to be 10 feet tall. Its seeds can be eaten like nuts.